IRREGULAR VOWEL COMBINATIONS

ô

o͝o

o͞o

ĕ

ā

Name ______________________ Date ______________________

CHECK LIST

au

au=ô

cause

haul

maul

Paul

pause

Additional Words that have this au *sound:*

auditorium
August
Australia
author
autograph
automat
automobile
autumn
caution
exhaust
fault
saucer
sausage

aught

aught=ôt

caught

taught

Additional Words that have this aught *sound:*

daughter
haughty......too proud of oneself
onslaught....attack
slaughter.....killing of an animal

ought

ought=ôt

bought

brought

fought

ought

thought

Additional Words that have this ought *sound:*

sought after......in demand
drought...........long period of dry weather
wrought iron

Name ____________________ Date ____________________

ook	**ood**
book, brook, cook, shook, hook, look, took	good, stood, hood, wood
ook=ŏŏk	ood=ŏŏd

1. Open your [book / look / nook] to page 24.

2. The fish was caught with a [hook / look / nook] .

3. We [book / brook / shook] the bag and the frog fell out.

4. Our teacher [hook / took / book] us out to play.

5. We sat under a tree by the [brook / shook / look] .

6. Ann will [nook / look / cook] dinner for you and me.

7. [Cook / Look / Book] under the rug for the pin.

8. We will sit in the [look / hook / nook] and read a book.

Name ______________________ Date ______________________

ook

For those who print

1. you look

2. she can cook

For those who use cursive.

1. you look

2. she can cook

Name ________________________ Date ________________________

I.

b*ull*dog

ull

bull
full
pull

ull=ŏŏl

1. The bag is __________ of candy.	pull full
2. __________ the [elephant] over here.	Pull Bull Full
3. Did you see the __________ fight?	full pull bull

II.

ould

could
would
should

ould=ŏŏd

The pupil reads the first part of the sentence and decides how to finish it.
If the pupil cannot write the rest of the sentence the instructor writes it for him/her.
When all the sentences are finished the pupil reads all the completed sentences.

1. Paul could win the race if ______________________________

2. Would you please get ______________________________

3. We should help our ______________________________

Name ______________________ Date ______________________

ull

For those who print

1. we pull

2. it is full

For those who use cursive.

1. we pull

2. it is full

Name ______________________ Date ______________________

CHECK LIST

oo

oo=ŏŏ

book	hood
brook	look
cook	nook
crook	shook
foot	stood
good	took
hook	wood

Additional words that have this oo *sound:*

football	footstep
foothold	good-bye
footlight	goodness
footlocker	hooky
footnote	soot.....a black dust-like material
footprint	woof....barking sound of dog family
footrest	wool

ould

ould=ŏŏd

would

could

should

ull

ull=ŏŏl

bull

full

pull

Additional words that have this ull *sound:*

bully

pulley.....a wheel with a v-shaped rim by which a rope turns it

pullet......a young hen

Name ______________________ Date ______________________

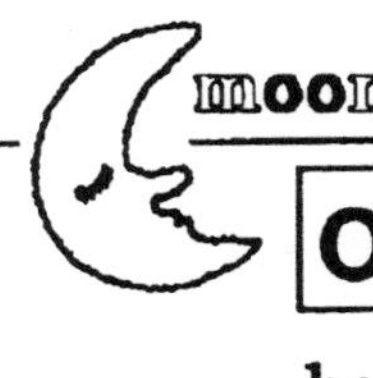

oo	oon	ool
boo coo moo zoo	moon spoon noon soon	cool spool fool pool tool
oo=o͞o	oon=o͞on	ool=o͞ol

1. The man said the [moon / noon / soon] is made of cheese.

2. I will get the [pool / tool / cool] and fix my bike.

3. We can go to the [boo / zoo / coo] today.

4. I like to dive into the [tool / pool / fool] when it is not too cool.

5. Dan will meet us today at [soon / loon / noon] .

6. Did Jim [pool / fool / cool] you with his new trick?

7. Soon the  will eat with a [soon / spoon / noon] .

8. A [loose / noose / moose] is a big animal.

Name ______________________ Date ______________________

oon

For those who print

1. It is noon

2. see you soon

For those who use cursive.

1. It is noon

2. see you soon

Name ______________________ Date ______________________

I.

soup
croup
group

oup = $\bar{oo}$p

The pupil reads the first part of the sentence and decides how to finish it.
If the pupil cannot write the rest of the sentence the instructor writes it for him/her.
When all the sentences are finished the pupil reads all the completed sentences.

1. **This soup is** ______________________

2. **A group of us went to** ______________________

3. **My** ______________ **has the croup.**

II.

All the following scrambled words have the oo sound.
Rearrange the letters to make a word.

lopo	osup	romo
________	________	________
grpou	olof	nono
________	________	________

Name ______________________ Date ______________________

oup

For those who print

1. hot soup
2. a group

For those who use cursive.

1. hot soup
2. a group

Name ______________________ Date ______________________

H I D E 'N S E E K

Draw a line around the hidden picture and write the number on it.

1. goose	4. broom	7. boot
2. hoop	5. spoon	8. moose
3. spool	6. moon	9. noose

Name ______________________ Date ______________________

ew

dew
new

chew
crew
flew
knew
screw
stew
threw

ew=$\overline{oo}$

1. The plane [dew / flew / knew] with a crew of five.

2. Mom bought me a [flew / new / knew] coat today.

3. Did the dog [chew / brew / threw] on the big bone?

4. Small drops of [dew / drew / new] were on the grass.

5. Mike [brew / stew / threw] the ball to Pat.

6. Do you like to eat [chew / stew / screw] ?

7. Rick [crew / knew / drew] a funny face on his cap.

8. I will [brew / flew / crew] some tea for you.

Name ______________________ Date ______________________

ew

For those who print

1. It is new

2. they flew

For those who use cursive.

1. It is new

2. they flew

Name ______________________ Date ______________________

I. Write the missing letters on the blanks.

1. We ate _____ew for supper. st fl ch

2. Ann _____ew the ball to Paul. dr thr ch

3. It is not raining but there is some _____ew. d dr cr

4. We will not eat the _____oup now. gr s cr

   It is too hot.

5. Our _____oup will camp here tonight. cr s gr

6. Rick is sick at home today.

   He has the _____oup. gr cr s

II.

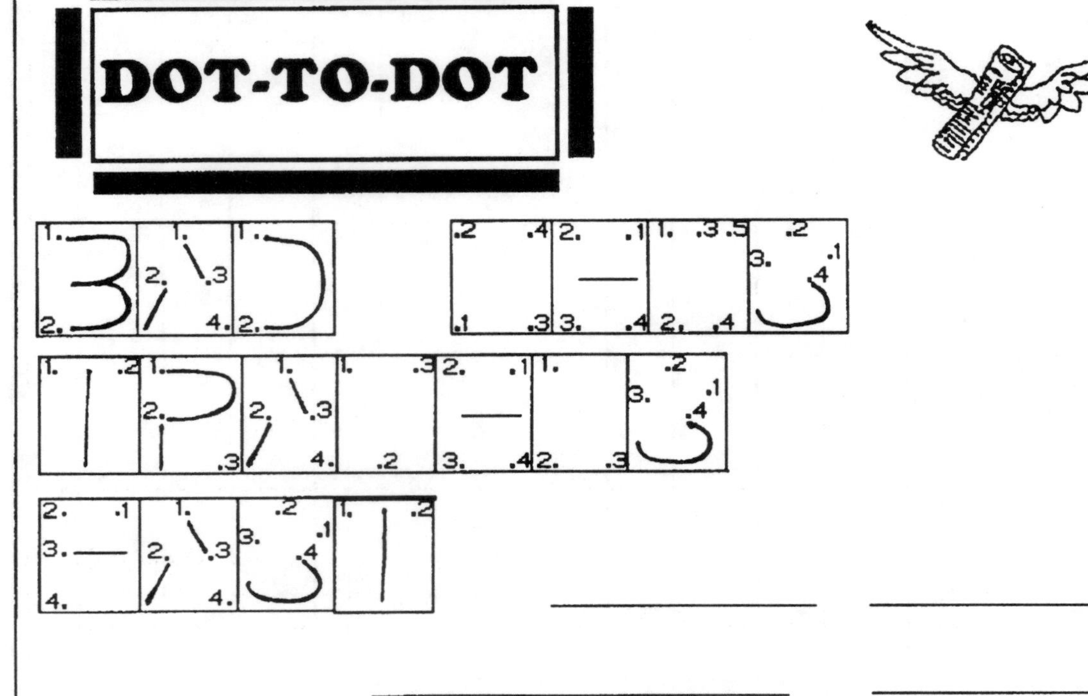

Name ______________________ Date ______________________

I.

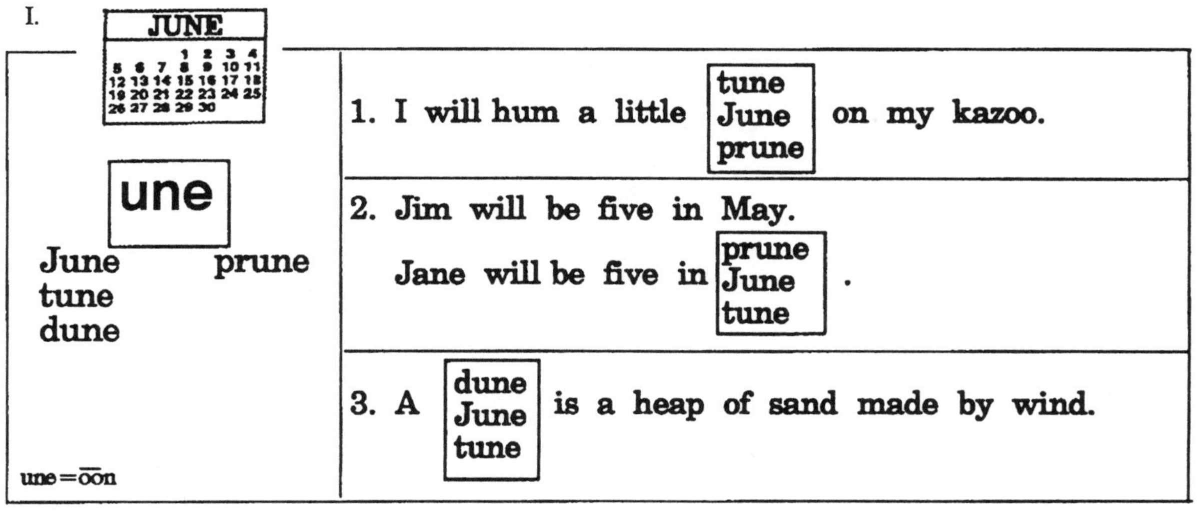

JUNE

			1	2	3	4
5	6	7	8	9	10	11
12	13	14	15	16	17	18
19	20	21	22	23	24	25
26	27	28	29	30		

une

June
tune
dune
prune

une = $\overline{oo}$n

1. I will hum a little [tune / June / prune] on my kazoo.
2. Jim will be five in May.
   Jane will be five in [prune / June / tune] .
3. A [dune / June / tune] is a heap of sand made by wind.

II.

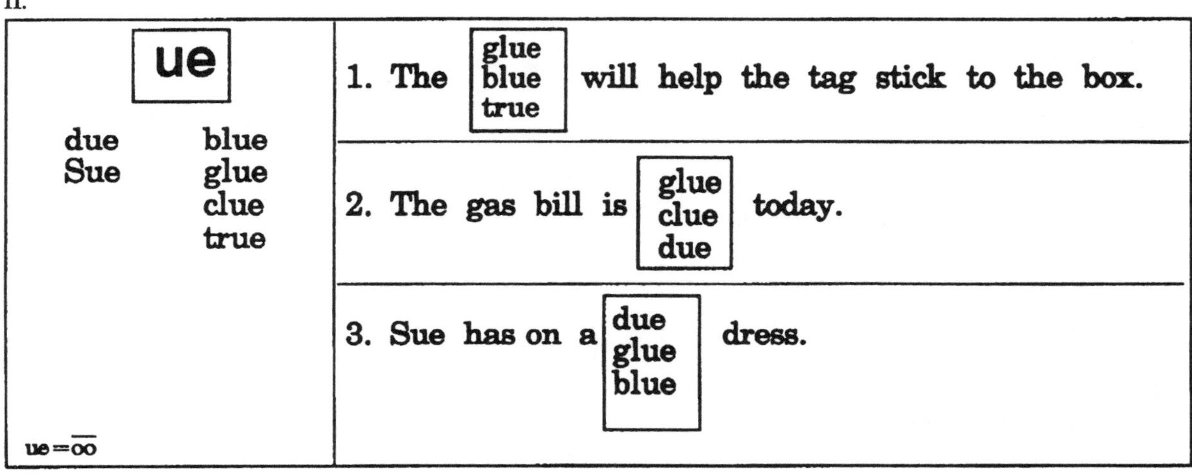

ue

due
Sue
blue
glue
clue
true

ue = $\overline{oo}$

1. The [glue / blue / true] will help the tag stick to the box.
2. The gas bill is [glue / clue / due] today.
3. Sue has on a [due / glue / blue] dress.

III.

fruit

uit **uise**

suit
fruit
bruise
cruise

uit = $\overline{oo}$t
uise = $\overline{oo}$z

1. We grew a lot of [suit / fruit] this summer.
2. Dan had a new blue [fruit / suit] for the wedding.
3. Did you [bruise / cruise] your foot?

Name ______________________

Date ______________________

ue

For those who print

1. it is blue

2. we will glue

For those who use cursive.

1. it is blue

2. we will glue

Name ____________________ Date ____________________

uit

For those who print

1. new suit

2. good fruit

For those who use cursive.

1. new suit

2. good fruit

Name ______________________ Date ______________________

I.

Each underlined word has the <u>ue</u> sound as in <u>blue.</u> Together with the context clues, the student should try to decode the underlined word and read the complete sentence.	
1. A <u>flue</u> is a pipe or tube that lets smoke out.	flue
2. The men fought a <u>duel</u> at sunrise.	duel
3. Do not be <u>cruel</u> to animals.	cruel

II.

Each underlined word has the <u>ui</u> sound as in <u>fruit.</u> Together with the context clues, the student should try to decode the underlined word and read the complete sentence.	
1. Jan fell and got a <u>bruise</u> on her arm.	bruise
2. We will go on a big boat for our <u>cruise</u> to Mexico.	cruise
3. Do you like <u>juice</u> with your meal?	juice

III.

Draw a line around the word or words on the right that <u>rhyme</u> with the word on the left.

new	blue	soup	chew	noon
June	tune	prune	suit	jean
zoo	zap	stew	hoop	glue
boot	fruit	boat	root	pool

In A Big Stew

"I'll cook something good," I said to friend Ann.
So I got out a spoon and a huge old black pan.

We looked in the cookbook to try something new.
And ended up making a big pot of stew.

As I hummed a soft <u>tune</u> I threw in a <u>prune,</u>
A slice of fat <u>goose</u> and some strawberry <u>juice.</u>

I shook in some salt, black pepper, and spice.
I even threw in a little brown rice.

And when I was through with making the stew,
I gave some to Ann and tried the stew, too.

But a look at Ann's face and I instantly knew
That Ann was not keen on this something called "stew."

Now I have not a clue as to what I should do.
As to what I should do with this huge pot of stew.

SAY!! How would you like to come over for lunch?
I'll even throw in a glass of pink punch!

Name ____________________ Date ____________________

CHECK LIST

oo

$oo = \overline{oo}$

boot	fool	moon	spool
boom	goose	moose	spoon
bloom	gloom	noon	stool
broom	groom	noose	stoop
coop	hoop	moose	toot
cool	hoot	pool	zoo
doom	loom	room	zoom
drool	loon	root	
droop	loop	soon	
food	loose	school	

Additional words that have this oo *sound:*

booby prize	goofy
booby trap	noodle
boost	poodle
choose	roost
doodad	rooster
doodle	woozy
gooey	yoo-hoo

ou

$ou = \overline{oo}$

croup

group

soup

Additional words that have this ou *sound:*

cougar......mountain lion. Member of the cat family
coupon
crouton.....toasted cube of dried bread used in soups and salads
louver...... an opening with slanted boards
mouton......sheep's fur made to look like beaver

ew

$ew = \overline{oo}$

brew	flew	threw
chew	knew	
crew	new	
dew	screw	
drew	stew	

Additional words that have this ew *sound :*

jewelry
newspaper
screwdriver
stewardess

Name ______________________ Date ______________________

CHECK LIST

ue

ue = $\overline{oo}$

blue glue

clue Sue

due true

flue

Additional words that have this ue *sound :*

cruel
duel

u_e

u_e = $\overline{oo}$

June

prune

tune

Additional words that have this u_e *sound :*

dune........a sand hill formed by the wind
dupe........trick, deceive
lube.........oil used to make machinery run smoothly
rule
tube

ui

ui = $\overline{oo}$

fruit

suit

Additional words that have this ui *sound :*

bruise
cruise
juice
recruit

Name ______________________ Date ______________________

feather

ead	ealth	eath	eather
head dead read bread dread tread thread spread ead = ĕd	health wealth ealth = ĕlth	death breath eath = ĕth	feather leather weather eather = ĕther

1. We will get a loaf of wheat ________ at the store.	dread bread tread
2. Did the ________ map show snow?	weather leather feather
3. The cold air made her ________ look like steam.	breath bread
4. We ________ butter and jam on our bread.	thread spread dread
5. Eat good food and it will make your ________ better.	wealth health
6. The bird has one big white ________.	feather leather weather
7. The book was so good I ________ it three times.	head read dead
8. Did you use brown ________ on your leather jacket?	dread tread thread

Name ______________________ Date ______________________

ead

For those who print

1. on his head

2. wheat bread

For those who use cursive.

1. on his head

2. wheat bread

Name ______________________ Date ______________________

Draw a picture for each word.

head	thread
bedspread	feather
nice weather	sweater

Name ____________________ Date ____________________

CHECK LIST

ea=ĕ

ea

bread	lead	weather
breath	leather	
dead	read	
death	spread	
feather	thread	
head	tread	
health	wealth	

Additional words that have this ea *sound :*

already	meadow	sweat
breakfast	measure	sweater
headache	peasant	threat
heavy	pleasant	treasure
instead	ready	weapon
jealous	steady	

Name ______________________ Date ______________________

eigh	eight	ein
weigh sleigh	eight freight weight	vein rein
eigh = ā	eight = āt	ein = ān

Before starting the exercise below explain these definitions:
1. rein.........a long narrow strap by which to guide an animal
2. sleigh......a carriage mounted on runners for use on snow or ice, pulled by one or more horses
3. freight.....goods carried by a vehicle

1. We can ship this [freight / eight] by train, track, or plane.

2. Blood flows through the [reins / veins] to the ♥ (heart).

3. Dan is [weight / eight] years old today.

4. How much do you [weigh / weight] ?

5. Before the race started the man took the [reins / veins] in his hands.

6. From far off we could hear the [weigh / sleigh] bells.

7. The nurse put my [eight / weight] on the chart.

Name ____________________

Date ____________________

eight

For those who print

1. he is eight

2. your weight

For those who use cursive.

1. he is eight

2. your weight

Name ______________________ Date ______________________

I. Put the letter that explains the meaning of the word on the blank space.

A. The number after seven	_____	ate
B. Past tense of eat	_____	eight
A. How heavy something is	_____	weight
B. To delay	_____	wait
A. A strap to guide an animal	_____	rein
B. Drops of water falling on earth	_____	rain
A. A carriage on runners	_____	slay
B. To kill	_____	sleigh

II.

Dot-To-Dot

Name ______________________ Date ______________________

I.

eak steak break eak=ēk	Read these sentences. 1. This <u>steak</u> is good. 2. Let's have more <u>steak</u>. 3. Let's take a <u>break</u>. 4. Did Meg <u>break</u> the dish?

II.

Put the letter that explains the meaning on the blank space.

A. A slice of meat ______ stake

B. A post in the ground ______ steak

A. Come apart ______ break

B. Something that holds back a wheel ______ brake

A. Very good ______ great

B. A frame to hold a fire ______ grate

Name ______________________

Date ______________________

eak

For those who print

1. don't break

2. it's a steak

For those who use cursive.

1. don't break

2. it's a steak

Name ______________________ Date ______________________

CHECK LIST

ei=ā

ei

eight

freight

rein

sleigh

vein

weigh

weight

Additional words that have this ei *sound:*

beige...........pale brown
eighty
feign............pretend
heinous.........very wicked
lei................a wreath of flowers worn around the neck
neighbor
reign.............the period of power of a ruler
reindeer
sleighbell
veil

eak=āk

eak

break

steak

Additional word with the ea *sound:*

great

DIPHTHONGS

ou

oi

Name ______________________ Date ______________________

mouse

out	ouse	ound
out, bout, pout, scout, shout, spout	house, louse, mouse, blouse	bound, found, hound, pound, round, sound, ground
out=out	ouse=ous	ound=ound

1. The [house / mouse / blouse] hid in the hole in the wall.
2. I [bound / round / found] a dime on the ground.
3. The teapot had a small [spout / shout / scout] .
4. Do not [scout / shout / bout] so loud.
5. The birds flew [mouth / south] for the winter.
6. We sat on the [couch / slouch / grouch] to see TV.
7. Our teacher was very [proud / loud / cloud] of our class.
8. The [hound / round / sound] of the fire truck was very loud.

Name ______________________ Date ______________________

out

For those who print

1. come out

2. good scout

For those who use cursive.

1. come out

2. good scout

Name ______________________ Date ______________________

ouse

For those who print

1. a big house

2. a gray mouse

For those who use cursive.

1. a big house

2. a gray mouse

Name ______________________ Date ______________________

I.

Each underlined word has the **ou** sound as in **out.**
Together with the context clues, the student should try to decode the underlined word and read the complete sentence.

1. The mountain had a lot of snow on its peak.	mountain
2. Throw a penny into the fountain.	fountain
3. Today is a cloudy day.	cloudy
4. A thousand men fought in the battle.	thousand
5. Did you count how many books you have now?	count

II.

DOT-TO-DOT

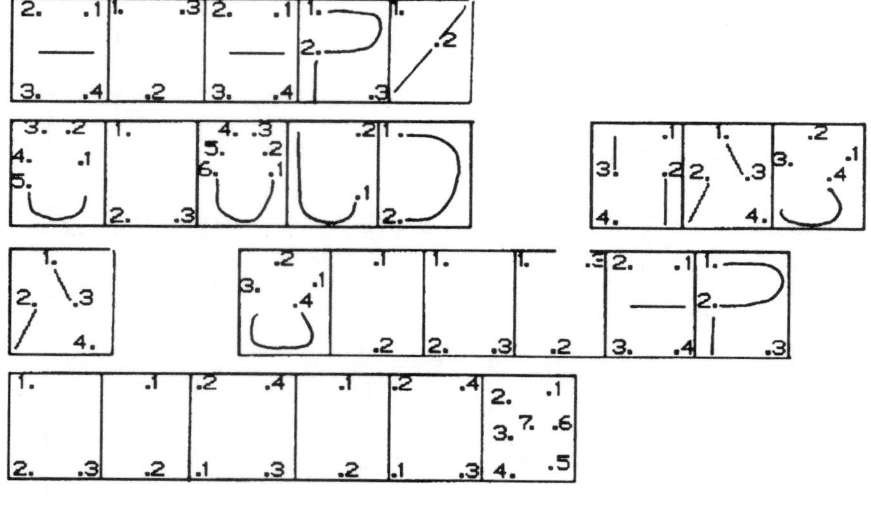

______________ ______________ ______________

______ ______________ ______________

Name ______________________ Date ______________________

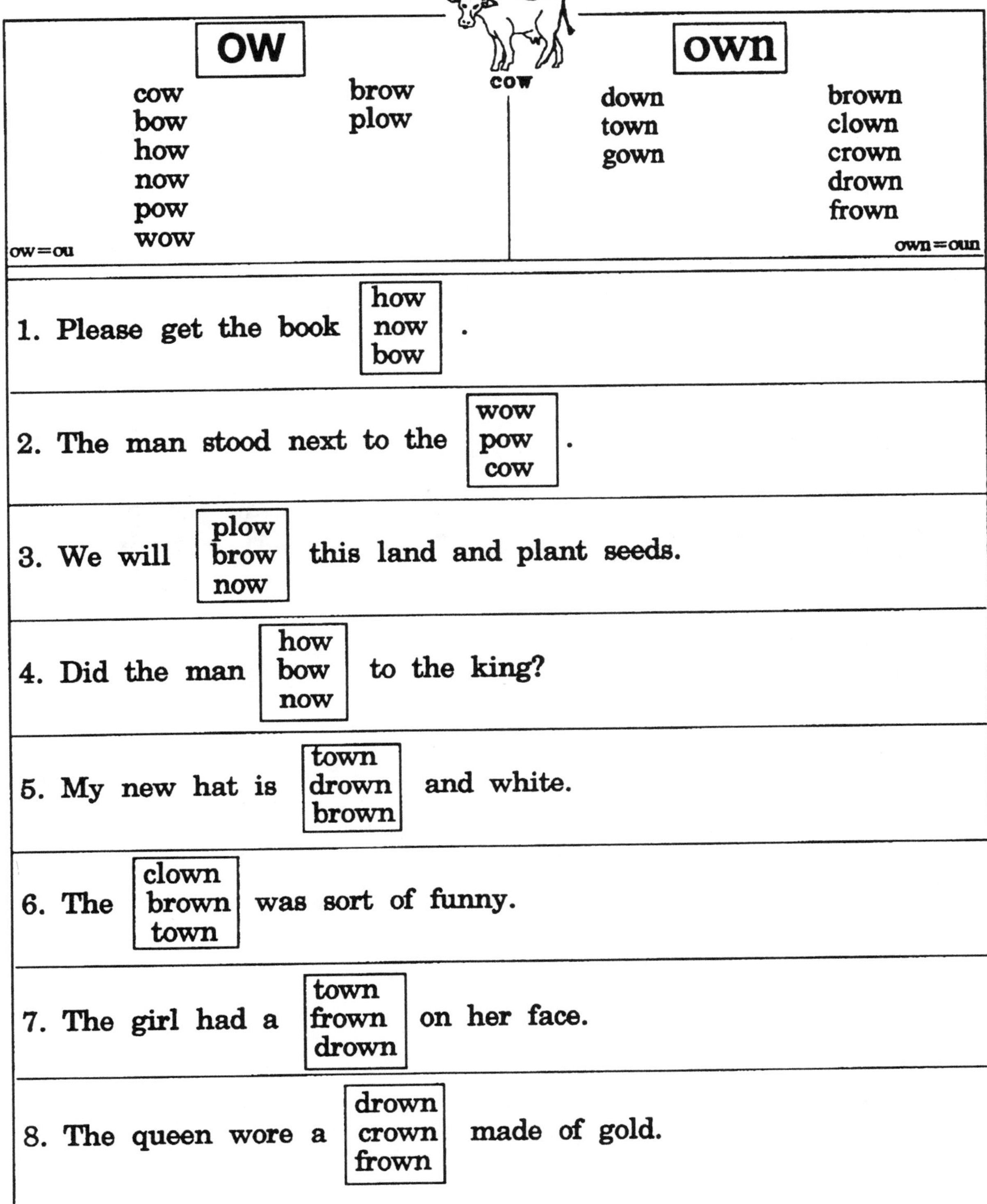

ow	own
cow bow how now pow wow brow plow	down town gown brown clown crown drown frown
ow=ou	own=oun

1. Please get the book [how / now / bow] .
2. The man stood next to the [wow / pow / cow] .
3. We will [plow / brow / now] this land and plant seeds.
4. Did the man [how / bow / now] to the king?
5. My new hat is [town / drown / brown] and white.
6. The [clown / brown / town] was sort of funny.
7. The girl had a [town / frown / drown] on her face.
8. The queen wore a [drown / crown / frown] made of gold.

Name ____________________ Date ____________________

ow

For those who print

1. stop now

2. see the cow

For those who use cursive.

1. stop now

2. see the cow

Name ______________________ Date ______________________

Each of the unfinished words below contains the <u>ow</u> sound as in *cow*.
The pupil reads the sentence and writes the missing letters to complete the word.

1. We must _____ ow the farm before it rains. p pl br

2. The _____ ow ate a lot of hay. n h c

3. Mom will let us go to the mall _____ ow. n s b

4. The man would not ____ ow to the king. h b s

5. The ____ own did a lot of funny tricks. cl dr cr

6. Dan will ride his horse into ____own today. g d t

7. My new jacket is ____ own and white. dr tr br

8. The king would not give up his ____own. dr cr br

9. The man was very upset.
   He had a _____ own on his face. dr fr t

10. Help us get the cat out of the well.
    It will _____own if we don't get it. dr cr cl

Name ______________________ Date ______________________

CHECK LIST

ow=ou

ow

bow	drown	town
brow	frown	wow
brown	gown	
cow	how	
clown	now	
crown	pow	
down	plow	

Additional words that have this ow *sound :*

crowd	power
drowsy	powder
flower	prowler
fowl	shower
growl	towel
howl	tower
owl	trowel

ou=ou

ou

blouse	hour	proud
bound	house	round
bout	loud	scour
couch	louse	scout
cloud	mouse	shout
flour	mouth	slouch
found	out	sound
grouch	pouch	sour
ground	pound	south
hound	pout	spout

Additional words that have this ou *sound:*

bough	flour
bounce	fountain
boundary	mount
bounty	mountain
cloudy	mouth
count	noun
county	thousand
doubt	

Name ______________________ Date ______________________

I.

coin

oil	oin	oint
boil broil coil spoil foil soil oil=oil	coin join oin=oin	joint point oint=oint

1. We will ________ this corn for a short time.	soil boil foil
2. Did you ________ the new club at school?	coin join
3. ________ to the place on the map where you are going.	Point Joint
4. This meat will ________ if it isn't kept cool.	coil foil spoil
5. We can put ________ around the meat. It will keep the meat cool.	foil boil coil
6. The ________ was made of pure gold.	coin join

II.

Say to the student, "Now that you know how the letters oi sound, see if you can figure out what the underlined words are."

1. We could not make out what the speaker was saying.

   The noise was very loud.

2. The food is nice and moist.

Name ______________________ Date ______________________

oil

For those who print

1. we will broil

2. it will spoil

For those who use cursive.

1. we will broil

2. it will spoil

Name ______________________________ Date ______________________________

Each underlined word has the ***oi*** sound as in ***oil***. Together with the context clues, the student should try to decode the underlined word and read the complete sentence.

1. Who is your choice for leader of the team?	choice
2. This cake is so good and moist.	moist
3. The class was very noisy today.	noisy
4. The oilcan is on the shelf.	oilcan
5. Did the poison kill the bugs?	poison

For 2 players. Use a spinning wheel that has numerals 1-6 on it. The pupil advances the number of spaces if he/she says the words correctly.

claw	spoil	food	spoil	flew	glue	STOP
paw						
suit	book	could	brown	mouse	cow	
					broil	
coin	haul	boil	law	tall	talk	jaw
all						
caught	fought	loop	oil	June	fruit	
					now	
GO	wood	town	house	join	point	hope

Name ______________________ Date ______________________

I.

boy
joy
Roy
toy

boy

oy=oi

1. The name of the little boy is [toy / Roy / joy].

2. Roy got a new [coy / toy / coy] for his first birthday.

3. The little [joy / coy / boy] took his new toy to school.

4. The storm was over.

There was a lot of [joy / Roy / toy] in the town.

II.

The student reads the first part of the sentence and decides how it should be finished. If he/she can't write the words, the instructor should print them. When all the sentences have been completed the student rereads the completed sentences.

1. My new toy is ______________________.

2. The boy gave his ______________________.

3. Roy is the name of ______________________.

4. Did you enjoy ______________________?

Name ______________________ Date ______________________

oy

For those who print

1. a good boy

2. a new toy

For those who use cursive.

1. a good boy

2. a new toy

Name ______________________________ Date ______________________________

I. ACROSS DOWN

II. Write a rhyming word for each word below:

boy	cow	wall	crown
________	________	________	________
paw	cook	talk	stew
________	________	________	________

Name ______________________ Date ______________________

CHECK LIST

oi=oi

oi

boil
broil
coin
coil
foil
hoist
join
joint
moist
noise
point
poise
soil
spoil
toil

Additional words that have this oi *sound:*

choice
foist...........to pass off as the real thing
loiter..........to linger idly
noisy
poison
oilcan
ointment
turquoise......greenish-blue semi-precious stone

oy=oi

oy

boy
coy
joy
Roy
toy

Additional words that have this oy *sound:*

loyal
oyster
royal
soybean
toybox
voyage

R-CONTROLLED VOWELS

är

ûr

ôr

ărr

ĕrr

îr ûr är âr

Name ______________________ Date ______________________

star ★

ark	ar	art
ark, bark, dark, mark, park, spark ark = ärk	car, bar, far, jar, tar, star ar = är	art, cart, dart, part, tart, chart, start art = ärt

1. My dog will not [dark / mark / bark] at you if you stand still.

2. Tom had a good [part / dart / art] in the school play.

3. Mark drew a [tar / star / far] on the book.

4. Hand me the [chart / start], please.

5. When we lit the fire cracker we saw a [dark / park / spark].

6. Dad put [far / tar / bar] on our driveway.

7. Put the food in the [cart / art / dart].

8. A [dark / bark / lark] is a small .

Name ______________________ Date ______________________

MARCH

S	M	T	W	TH	F	S
1	2	3	4	5	6	7
8	9	10	11	12	13	14
15	16	17	18	19	20	21
22	23	24	25	26	27	28
29	30	31				

ard	arch	arp
card hard lard ard=ärd	arch March starch arch=ärch	carp harp tarp arp=ärp

1. [Arch / March / Starch] is the third month of the year.

2. I cannot crush this rock. It is too [hard / card / lard].

3. We will put a [carp / harp / tarp] on the car. It will keep the snow off.

4. Mom will bake the pie crust with [hard / lard / card].

Each underlined word has the ar sound.
Together with the context clues, the student should be able to figure out the word.

1. The carpenter made a house out of wood. carpenter

2. Would you like to play a game of marbles? marbles

3. Do you grow beets in your garden? garden

4. We had a good time at the party. party

Name ____________________ Date ____________________

ark

For those who print

1. it is dark

2. in the park

For those who use cursive.

1. it is dark

2. in the park

Name ______________________ Date ______________________

1. Explain to the pupil that all the pictures in the exercise below begin with the same sound as the word ***arm***.
2. Read the following definitions to the pupil as you point to the picture:
   a. The arctic is the extremely cold region that lies north of the Arctic Circle.
   b. Argentina is a country in South America that is located between the South Pacific Ocean and the South Atlantic Ocean.
   c. An archway is an arch covering a passageway.
3. Next, the pupil names the picture and writes the name from the list.

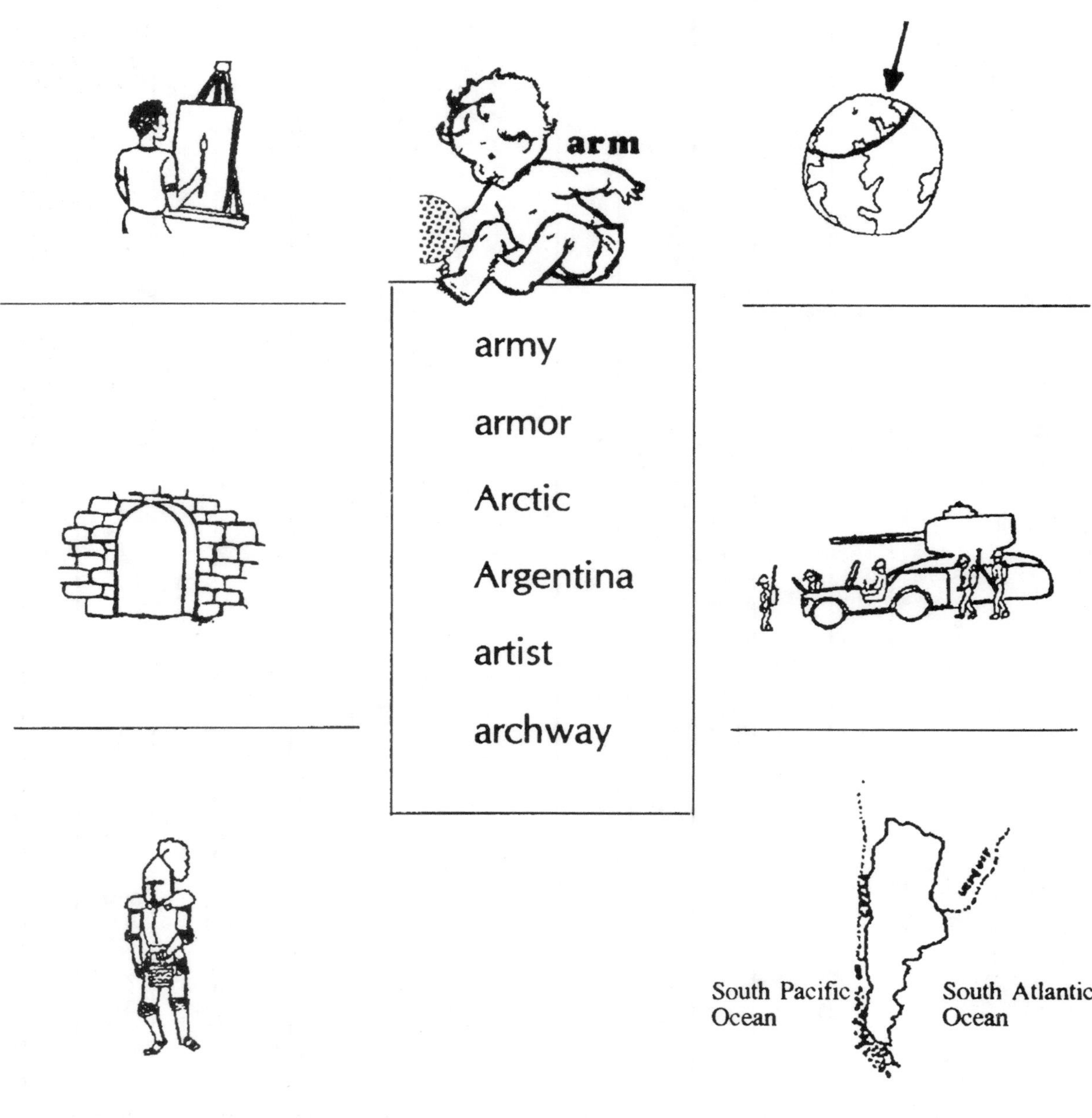

Name ______________________ Date ______________________

H I D E 'N S E E K

Draw a line around the hidden picture and write the number on it.

1. car
2. dart
3. star
4. jar
5. harp
6. lark
7. cart
8. card

Name ______________________ Date ______________________

CHECK LIST

ar

ar=är

ark	dart	part
arch	far	sharp
bar	hard	spark
bark	harp	star
car	jar	starch
card	lard	start
carp	lark	tar
cart	mark	tarp
chart	March	tart
dark	park	

Additional words that have this ar *sound :*

alarm	article	Mars
arbor	artist	marvel
arch	barnyard	marvelous
archway	carpenter	partner
arctic	carve	party
Argentina	farm	sardine
argue	garden	scarf
argument	harbor	sparkle
armor	harm	varnish
army	large	varsity
arsenal	marble	
Arthur	market	

Name ______________________ Date ______________________

ur	urp	urn	url
bur blur fur slur ur=ûr	burp slurp urp=ûrp	burn turn urn=ûrn	curl furl hurl url=ûrl

1. The ball player can [curl / hurl / furl] the ball far.
2. The fire will [burn / turn] for just a while.
3. The [slur / blur / fur] of the animal was very thick.
4. Please [turn / burn] the pancakes over.
5. Mom will [furl / curl / hurl] Barb's hair.
6. I could not read the book. It was all a [fur / bur / blur] .
7. A [bur / blur / slur] can stick your skin and hurt.
8. Do not [bur / slur / fur] your letters when you speak.

Name ______________________ Date ______________________

urn

For those who print

1.	2.
it will burn	we can turn

For those who use cursive.

1.	2.
it will burn	we can turn

Name ______________________________ Date ______________________________

turtle

Each underlined word has the ur sound as in turtle.
Together with the context clues, the student should try to decode the underlined word and read the complete sentence.

1. The turtle is a very slow animal.	turtle
2. We had a turkey sandwich for lunch.	turkey
3. Purple is a mix of red and blue.	purple
4. Mom bought a new curtain for the window.	curtain
5. Mom bought new furniture for my bedroom.	furniture

For 2 players. Use a spinning wheel that has numerals 1-6 on it. The pupil advances the number of spaces if he/she says the words correctly.

herb	blur	sir	dirt	chalk	raw	STOP
her						
blue	slaw	shirt	perk	small	turn	bur
						fur
stir	hall	hurl	clerk	draw	crawl	fir
all						
curl	verb	skirt	burn	jerk	twirl	girl
						saw
GO	germ	term	slur	taught	March	soon

Name ______________________ Date ______________________

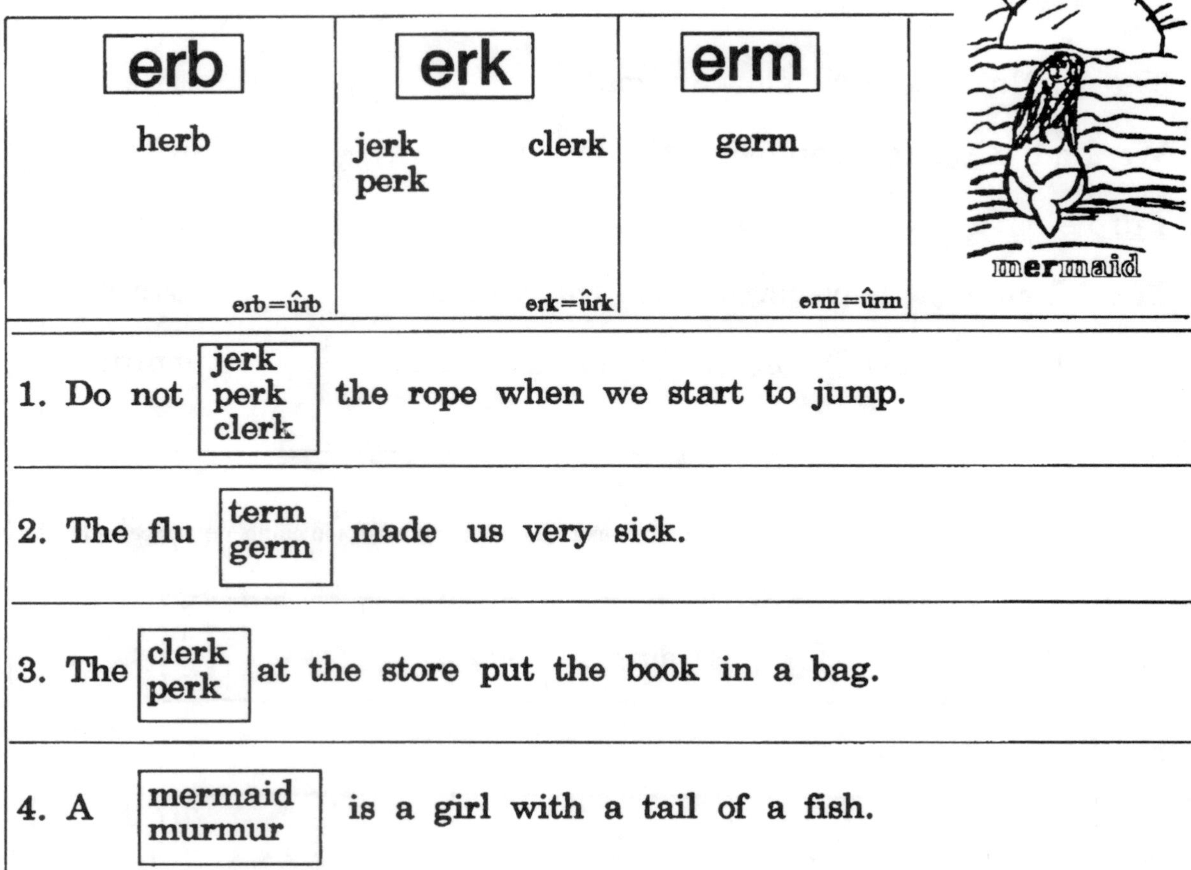

erb	erk	erm	
herb	jerk clerk perk	germ	mermaid
erb=ûrb	erk=ûrk	erm=ûrm	

1. Do not [jerk / perk / clerk] the rope when we start to jump.

2. The flu [term / germ] made us very sick.

3. The [clerk / perk] at the store put the book in a bag.

4. A [mermaid / murmur] is a girl with a tail of a fish.

Each underlined word has the er sound as in mermaid.
Together with the context clues, the student should try to decode the underlined word and read the complete sentence.

1. The U.S. team had a perfect score. perfect

2. A termite is a bug that likes to eat wood. termite

3. It was 32° on the thermometer. thermometer

4. Did you ever eat strawberry sherbet? sherbet

Name ______________________ Date ______________________

erk

For those who print

1. I am a clerk

2. don't jerk

For those who use cursive.

1. I am a clerk

2. don't jerk

Name ______________________ Date ______________________

I.

DEFINITIONS

1. Something that can make us sick ____ herd
2. Someone who helps us in a store ____ herb
3. Something we can grow in a garden ____ clerk
4. A sharp twist ____ germ
5. A lot of animals ____ jerk

II.

DOT-TO-DOT

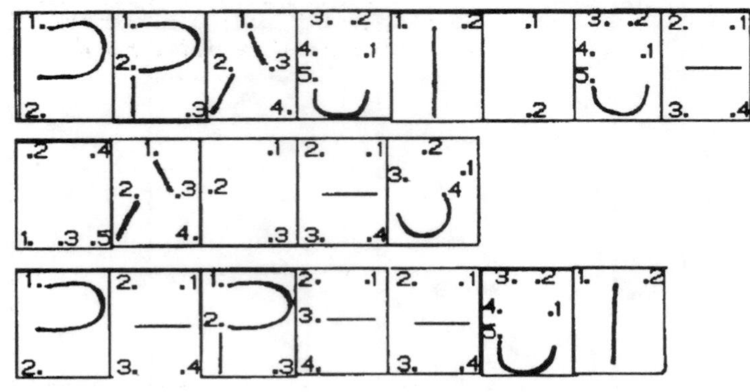

______________ ______________ ______________

Name ____________________ Date ____________________

I.

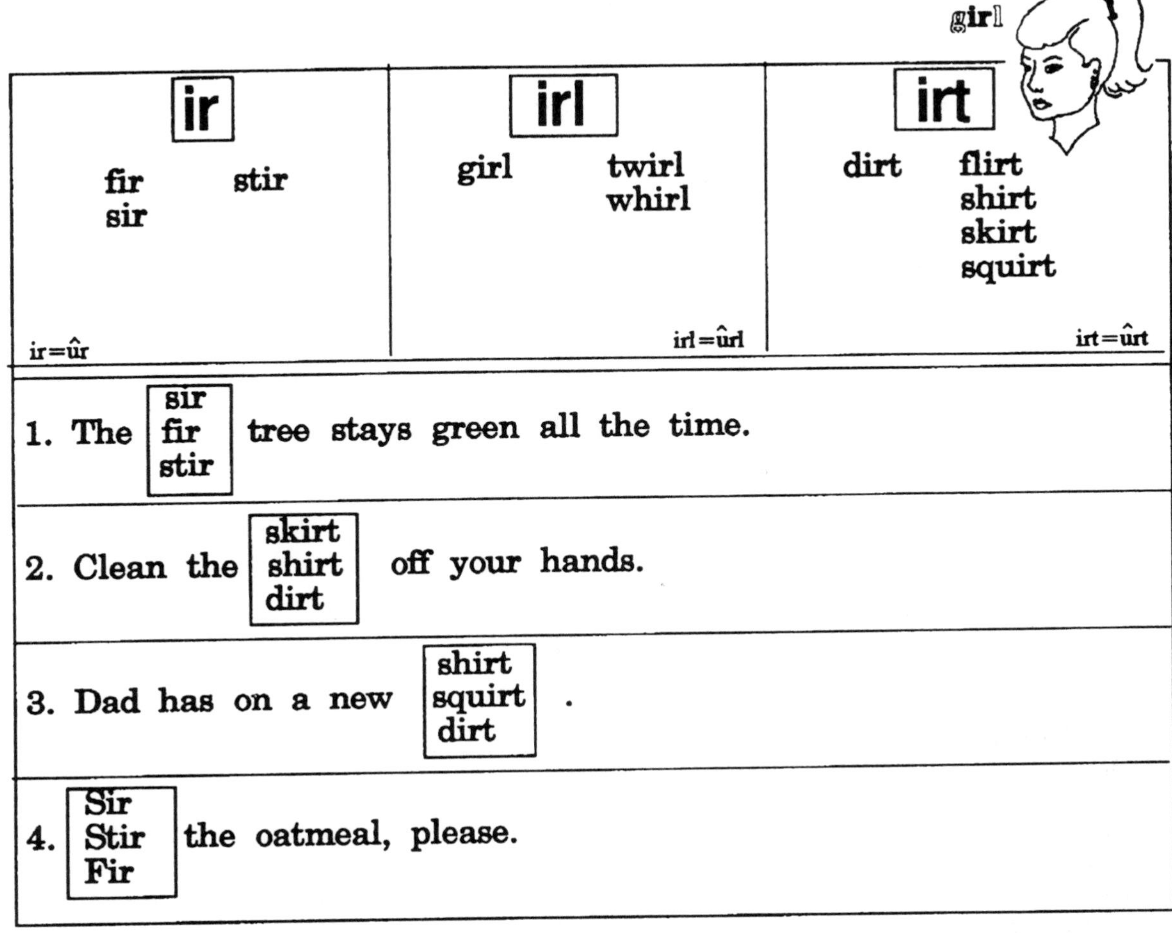

girl

ir	irl	irt
fir stir sir	girl twirl whirl	dirt flirt shirt skirt squirt
ir=ûr	irl=ûrl	irt=ûrt

1. The [sir / fir / stir] tree stays green all the time.

2. Clean the [skirt / shirt / dirt] off your hands.

3. Dad has on a new [shirt / squirt / dirt] .

4. [Sir / Stir / Fir] the oatmeal, please.

II. The student reads the first part of the sentence and decides how it should be finished. If he/she can't write the words, then the instructor should print it out. When all the sentences have been completed the student rereads them.

1. Did you see the girl twirl the ____________________?

2. "Yes, sir," said the little boy to ____________________.

3. The squirt gun ____________________.

4. Her new skirt ____________________.

ir

For those who print

1. yes, sir

2. let me stir

For those who use cursive.

1. yes, sir

2. let me stir

Name ______________________ Date ______________________

I.

UNSCRAMBLERS

ris	rigl	drti
________	________	________
rtis	tishr	sritk
________	________	________

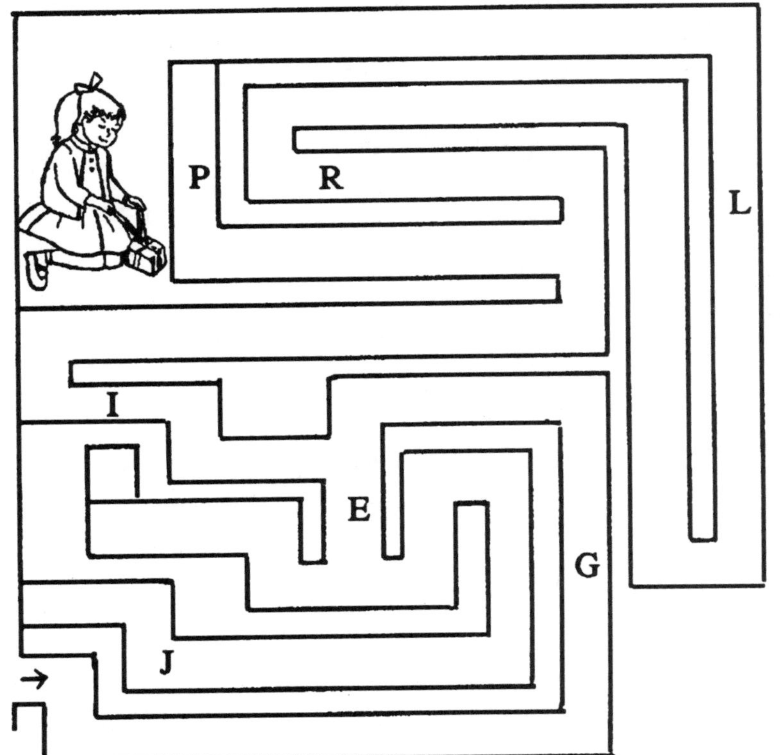

II.

A-MAZE-ING

___ ___ ___ ___

Name ______________________ Date ______________________

I.

wor

word
worm
work
world
worth

world

wor=wûr

1. How much is that old car ________ ?	word world worth
2. Do you ________ at the mall?	work word worth
3. We call our ________ EARTH.	word world work
4. Larry put a ________ on the hook for bait.	worth worm work
5. Jerry could read every ________ in the book.	work world word

II.

On the blank line, put the number of the word on the left that matches the definition.

1. workbench	________	someone who works very hard
2. workbag	________	something in which a pupil does homework
3. workbook	________	a place where work is done
4. workhorse	________	a table at which a person works
5. workroom	________	something that holds things a person works with

Name ______________________ Date ______________________

wor

For those who print

1.	2.
they work	it's a worm

For those who use cursive.

1.	2.
they work	it's a worm

Name ________________________ Date ________________________

I.

Draw a line from a word on the left to a word on the right that rhymes.

work	herd
girl	jerk
stir	curb
word	germ
herb	fur
worm	curl

II.

Draw a line around all the words on the right that have the same vowel sound as the word on the left.

work	her	cart	stir	fur
perk	worm	girl	turn	here
word	for	curb	dirt	herb
shirt	germ	fir	curl	world
worth	surf	third	store	clerk
burn	bark	verb	firm	work

Name ______________________ Date ______________________

CHECK LIST

ir

ir=ûr

dirt
shirt
fir
skirt
girl
squirt
sir
twirl
stir
whirl

Additional words that have this ir *sound:*

birch
bird
birdbath
birdhouse
birthday
chirp
circus
dirty
firm
first
giraffe
third
thirsty
thirty

er

er= ûr

germ
perk
her
term
herb
verb
jerk

Additional words that have this er *sound:*

certain
expert
fern
geranium
herd
hermit
kernel
mercy
merchant
per cent
perch
perfect
performance
perhaps
personality
servant
sherbet
thermometer
thermostat

ur

ur=ûr

bur
curl
slur
burn
fur
slurp
burp
furl
turn
blur
hurl

Additional words that have this ur *sound :*

burden
burglar
church
churn
curb
curtain
curve
disturb
furnace
furniture
hurricane
hurry
jury
murmur
nurse
purchase
purple
purpose
purse
Saturday
turkey
turnip
turnpike
turtle

wor

wor=wûr

word
world
worm
worth
work

Additional words that have this wor *sound :*

word-for-word
workbench
workbook
world-wide
wormwood
worry
worship
worst
worthy

Name ______________________ Date ______________________

I.

orn

born
corn
horn
torn
worn

orn = ôrn

1. This coat is old and [worn / corn / horn] .

corn

2. We grew this [born / corn / born] in our garden.

3. Don't toot the [worn / torn / horn] or you will wake the baby.

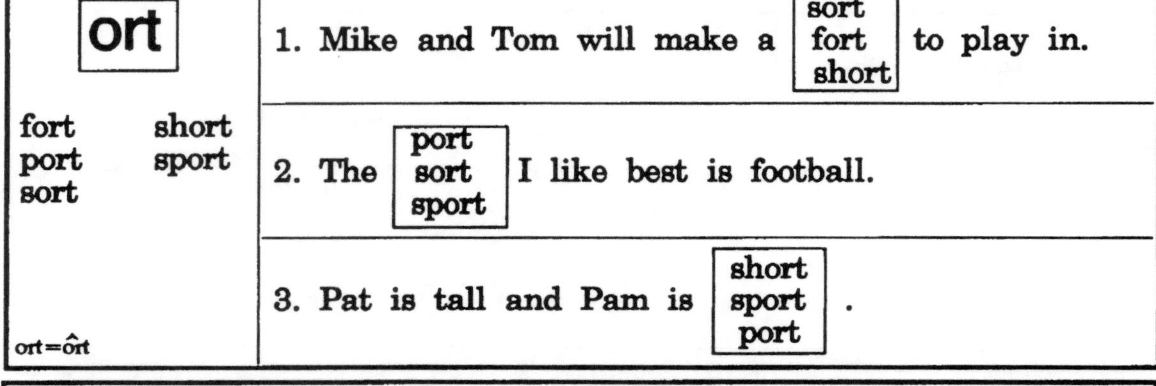

II.

ort

fort
port
sort
short
sport

ort = ôrt

1. Mike and Tom will make a [sort / fort / short] to play in.

2. The [port / sort / sport] I like best is football.

3. Pat is tall and Pam is [short / sport / port] .

III.

orm

form
dorm
storm

orm = ôrm

1. We had a snow [storm / form / dorm] here this morning.

2. Mom will fill out this [dorm / form / storm] and I will take it to school.

IV.

ork

cork
fork
pork
stork

ork = ôrk

1. You should place the [stork / fork] on the left of the plate.

2. The [pork / stork / cork] is a bird with a long bill and long legs.

Name ______________________ Date ______________________

orn

For those who print

1. it is torn
2. is it worn

For those who use cursive.

1. it is torn
2. is it worn

Name ______________________ Date ______________________

Each underlined word has the or sound as in *orchestra*.
Together with the context clues, the student should try to decode the underlined word and read the complete sentence.

1. **Ned will play his horn in the school orchestra.** orchestra

2. **An orange has a lot of good juice.** orange

3. **The tornado hit our town and tore down our homes.** tornado

4. **Please put the books back in the right order.** order

5. **I will tell you a story if you sit still.** story

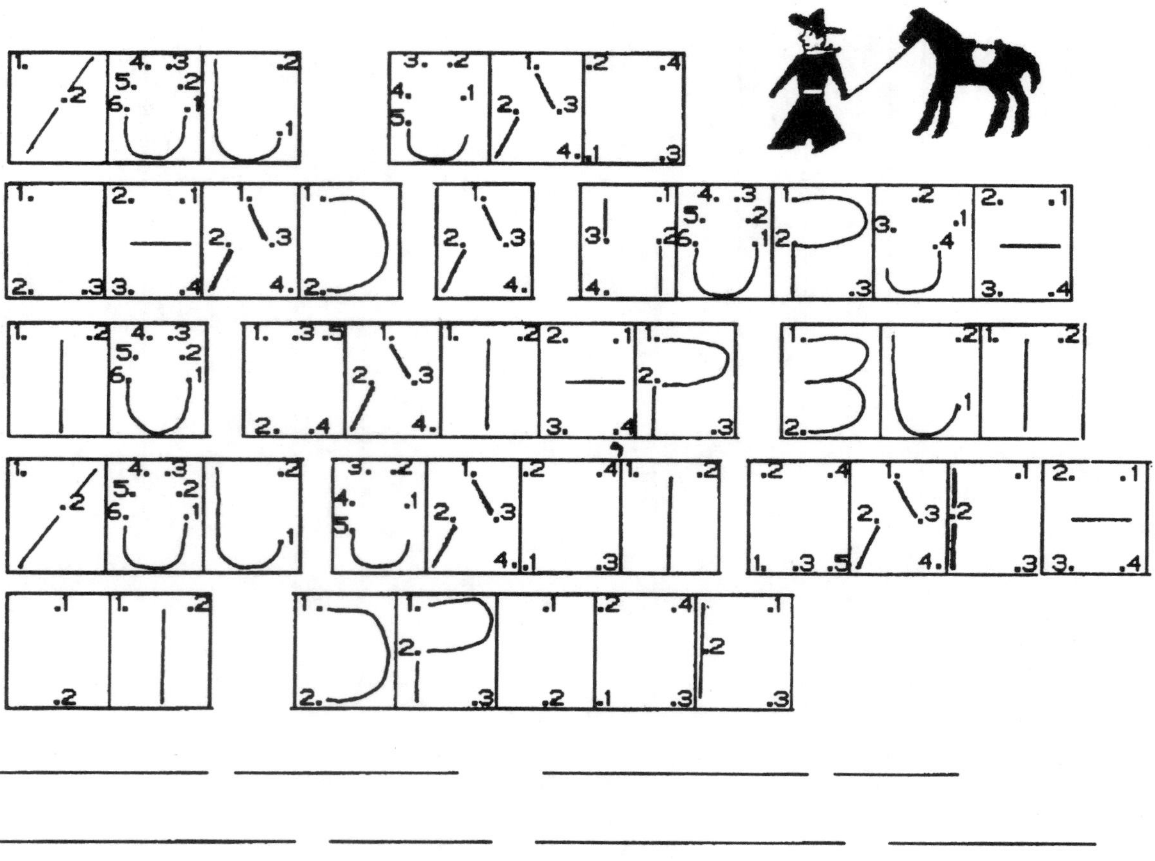

______ ______ ______ ______

______ ______ ______ ______

______ ______ ______ ______ ______

Name ______________________ Date ______________________

HIDE 'N SEEK

The following objects are hidden in the picture above:
Draw a line around the picture and write the number on it.

1. horn
2. north
3. forty
4. corn
5. stork
6. torpedo
7. fork
8. horse
9. orange

Name ______________________ Date ______________________

war

wart hog

war
warn
warp
wart
warm

war=wôr

Before starting this exercise read the following definitions:
to warp means to bend an object out of shape
a wart hog is a wild hog that has wartlike growths on each side of its face and has tusks

1. This is a __________ coat.	warm warp wart
2. That hot pan will __________ if you cool it too soon.	war warn warp
3. Did Jerry __________ the crowd about the ice storm?	wart warn warp
4. The men came home from the __________ .	warm warn war
5. The __________ hog has big warts on its face.	wart warn warp
6. The __________ of the fire made us feel better.	wart warmth warp

Name ______________________ Date ______________________

war

For those who print

1. we are warm

2. it will warp

For those who use cursive.

1. we are warm

2. it will warp

Name ______________________________ Date ______________________________

a b c d e f g h i j k l m n o p q r s t u v w x y z

I. Put the words that are in the box in alphabetical order.

warp	ward	warn	wart	warm

1. ____________________

2. ____________________

3. ____________________

4. ____________________

5. ____________________

II.

The student reads the first part of the sentence and decides how it should be finished. If he/she can't write it, then the instructor should print it out. When all the sentences have been completed the student rereads them.

1. The war ______________________________ .

2. We will warn ______________________________ .

3. The ______________________________ is nice and warm.

4. The ______________________________ had war paint on his face.

5. The wart on his hand ______________________________ .

Name ______________________ Date ______________________

CHECK LIST

or

or=ôr

born	porch
corn	scorch
cork	short
dorm	sport
fort	storm
fork	stork
horn	torn
port	torch
pork	worn

Additional words that have this or *sound :*

border	morning	orbit	orient
cord	New York	orchard	orphan
corner	normal	orchestra	port
for	north	order	story
forty	Norway	organ	tornado
horse	orange	organization	torpedo

war

war=wôr

war

warm

warmth

warn

warp

Additional words that have the ar *sound:*

warble..........to sing as birds sing
warden..........the head of a prison
warranty........a promise backing up a claim
Warsaw........ a city in the country of Poland

Name ____________________ Date ____________________

I.

arrow

arrow

narrow
sparrow

arry

carry
marry
Harry
Larry

ar(r)=ăr

1. I cannot get through here. This place is too [arrow / sparrow / narrow].
2. The [arrow / sparrow / narrow] is a small bird.
3. Please help me [Harry / carry / marry] this box, Larry.
4. Did Larry [Harry / marry] Pam?

II.

cherry

erry

berry
ferry
merry

cherry

Jerry
Kerry
Perry

er(r)=ĕr

* Before starting this exercise read these definitions
merry... joyful
ferry.... a boat used to carry people and goods across a river

1. The [ferry / berry / merry] boat took us across the lake.
2. I like [merry / ferry / cherry] pie the best.
3. [Kerry / Perry / Jerry] begins with the same sound as Paul.

Name ____________________

Date ____________________

err

For those who print

1. is he Larry
2. he is Jerry

For those who use cursive.

1. is he Larry
2. he is Jerry

Name ______________________ Date ______________________

I. Things That Go Together

pie   Christmas   boat   nest   arrow

1. bow and ______________________
2. sparrow and ______________________
3. Merry ______________________
4. cherry ______________________
5. ferry ______________________

II.

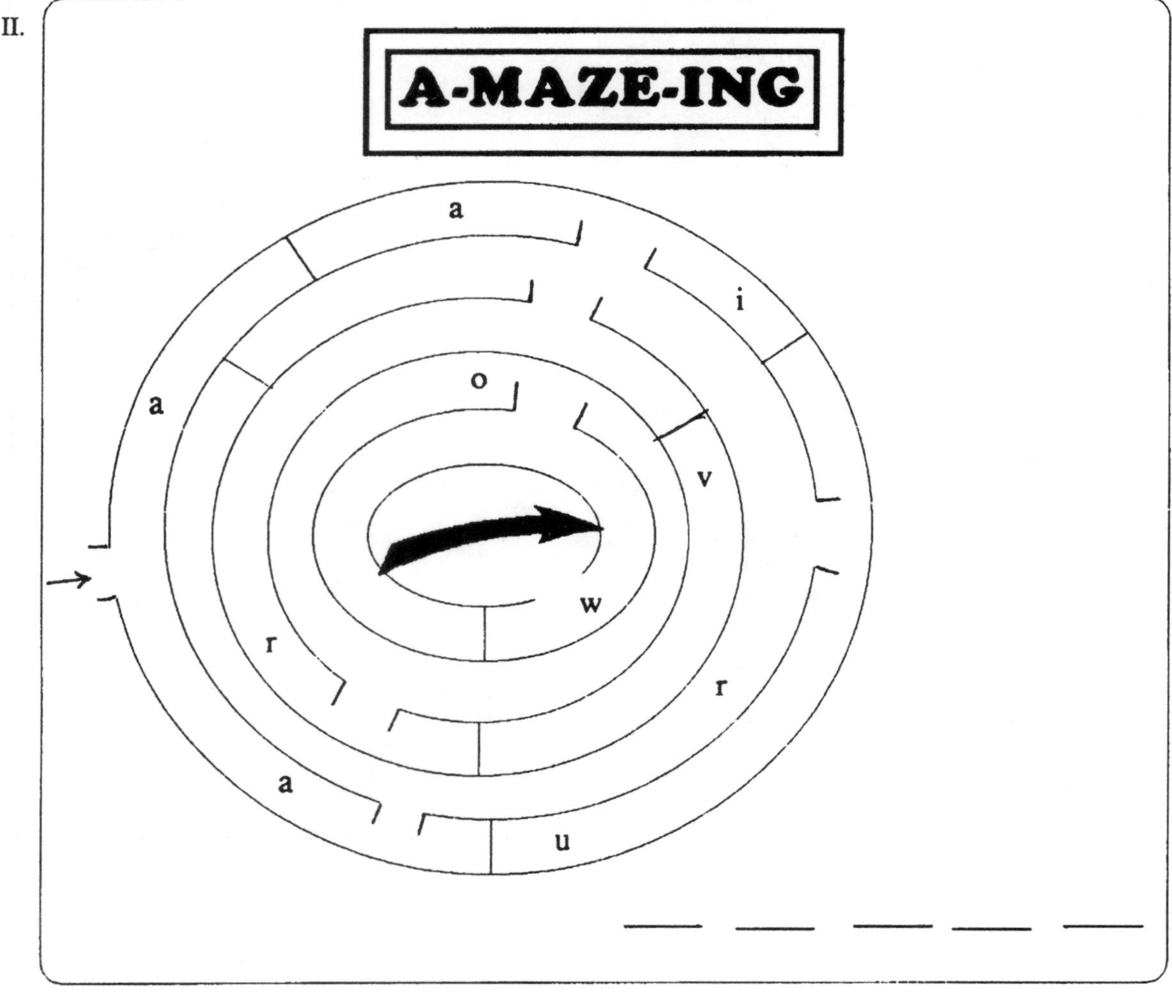

Name ______________________ Date ______________________

CHECK LIST

ar(r)=ăr

ar(r)

arrow

carry

Harry

Larry

marry

narrow

sparrow

Additional Words that have this ar(r) *sound:*

barracks........military living quarters
barracuda.......a large, savage fish from the waters north of Brazil
barrel
barricade........barrier made in a hurry for protection
barrier...........something that bars entrance
carriage
carrot
marriage
parrot

er(r)=ĕr

er(r)

berry

cherry

ferry

merry

Jerry

Kerry

Perry

Additional words that have this er(r) *sound:*

blueberry
cranberry
derrick
errand
error
ferris wheel
herring.............small fish that can be prepared for eating
terrible
terrify
territory
terry cloth

Name ______________________ Date ______________________

FOUR SOUNDS FOR **ear**

1. ear (îr) as in spear
2. ear (ûr) as in pearl
3. ear (är) as in heart
4. ear (âr) as in bear

I.

spear

dear, fear, hear, near, tear, year, spear, clear

ear=îr

1. Did you ________ the sound of the bell?	dear hear year
2. The sound of the bell was ________ .	year spear clear
3. Next ________ our class will go to New York.	year tear fear
4. Ann sat ________ Andy.	hear near tear

II.

pearl

pearl, Earl

earn, learn

ear=ûr

1. Mom bought Sue a ________ pin.	Earl pearl
2. I will ________ to play a brass horn.	earn learn
3. ________ is the name of the boy.	Pearl Earl
4. I can ________ a coin for helping Dad.	learn earn

Name ______________________ Date ______________________

(four Sounds for **ear** continued)

III.

heart

heart
hearty
hearth

1.	Did your __________ pound when you won?	heart hearty
2.	The __________ of the fireplace is brick.	hearty hearth
3.	We had some __________ soup for lunch.	hearth hearty

ear=är

IV.

bear

bear
pear
tear

1.	A __________ is good for a snack.	tear pear bear
2.	The box will __________ if you drop it.	tear bear
3.	The __________ has thick fur and a short tail.	pear tear bear

ear-âr

Name ______________________

Date ______________________

ear

For those who print

1. can you hear

2. it is clear

For those who use cursive.

1. can you hear

2. it is clear

Name ______________________

Date ______________________

ear

For those who print

1. earn it

2. learn it

For those who use cursive.

1. earn it

2. learn it

Name ______________________ Date ______________________

ear

For those who print

1. big heart

2. stone hearth

For those who use cursive.

1. big heart

2. stone hearth

Name ____________________ Date ____________________

ear

For those who print

1. a big bear
2. a small pear

For those who use cursive.

1. a big bear
2. a small pear

Name ______________________ Date ______________________

HIDE 'N SEEK

The following objects are hidden in the picture above.
Draw a line around the picture and write the number on it.

1. head	4. bread	7. thread
2. feather	5. peach	8. pearl
3. steak	6. spear	9. heart

Name ______________________ Date ______________________

CHECK LIST

ear

ear = îr

clear	sear
dear	shear
fear	spear
gear	tear
hear	year
near	

Additional words that have this **ear** *sound* :

appear
spearmint
weary

ear

ear = âr

bear

pear

tear

ear

ear = ûr

Earl

earn

learn

pearl

Additional words that have this **ear** *sound* :

early
earth
heard
hearse
search

ear

ear = är

heart

hearth

hearty

Additional word that has this **ear** *sound:*

hearken.....to listen carefully